D0463451

HOW **TIME** IS ON
YOUR **SIDE**

HOW **TIME** IS ON YOUR **SIDE**

BRIDGET WATSON PAYNE

CHRONICLE BOOKS
San Francisco

Text copyright © 2020 by Bridget Watson Payne.

Library of Congress Cataloging-in-Publication Data:

Names: Payne, Bridget Watson, author.
Title: How time is on your side / by Bridget Watson Payne.
Description: San Francisco : Chronicle Books, [2020] | Includes
   bibliographical references.
Identifiers: LCCN 2018045081 | ISBN 9781452171937 (hc : alk. paper)
Subjects: LCSH: Time management. | Time—Psychological aspects. |
   Time—Social aspects.
Classification: LCC HD69.T54 P39 2019 | DDC 650.1/1—dc23 LC
record available at https://lccn.loc.gov/2018045081

Manufactured in China.

MIX
Paper from
responsible sources
FSC™ C137129

Design by Vanessa Dina and Alma Kamal.

10 9 8 7 6 5 4 3 2 1

Chronicle books and gifts are available at special quantity discounts to corporations, professional associations, literacy programs, and other organizations. For details and discount information, please contact our premiums department at corporatesales@chroniclebooks.com or at 1-800-759-0190.

Chronicle Books LLC
680 Second Street
San Francisco, California 94107
www.chroniclebooks.com

TIME IS YOUR FRIEND

INTRODUCTION 8

BEFORE WE BEGIN 12

LET'S EMPOWER OURSELVES 20

THE THREE BIG CHANGES OF MIND-SET 30

ALL THE STUFF WE NEED TO DO 40

THE PROS AND CONS OF PRODUCTIVITY
THINKING 72

TIPS, TRICKS, AND LIFE HACKS 78

CONCLUSION 111

ACKNOWLEDGMENTS 114

BIBLIOGRAPHY 115

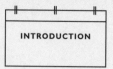

It is a truth universally acknowledged that no one in today's world has enough time. Everyone is too busy. Everyone is overwhelmed. No one feels they're devoting as much time as they'd like to their careers or their friends or their partners or their families or their creative pursuits or their social conscience. Let alone their own quiet inner selves.

A million opinion pieces and life-hack books have been written about productivity, about how to get more done in the not-enough-time we have.

And then a million other think pieces have been written suggesting we basically throw productivity out the window. Replace it with mindfulness. Replace it with minimalism. Replace it with self-care. Replace it with rest. Replace it with play.

But these ideals—wonderful and worthy though they are—in turn become just more occasions for self-loathing. Oh god, we think, now I'm not playing enough, I'm not meditating enough, I'm not purging my closets enough, I'm not taking enough bubble baths. What the hell is wrong with me?

The answer, of course, is nothing. And everything. We are all perfect exactly as we are. And, simultaneously, we are all profoundly flawed and infinitely improvable. That's the conundrum, the essential paradox of being human. How do we accept our glorious and broken selves just as we are, while also constantly striving for the good?

The demands of life are pressing in upon us. The jobs need doing. The children need raising. The marriages need tending. The world needs saving. We need to hold ourselves, and those around us, with the same tenderness with which we'd hold a tiny baby. While at the same time we need to fight for what is right with the tenacity of a full-grown adult human who isn't exhausted all the damn time.

We need to get going. We have big important things to do. And to do them we must get all the crap out of our way. Clear the underbrush. Banish the detritus. Muster our resources and get crystal clear about what's worth it and what's not. We must find the mix of practical tools and big ideas that allow us to make friends with time.

Yes, really, *friends*. **Time, it turns out, is not actually your enemy.** It's not against you. If time could want, it would probably want to be enough for you. Just like we all want to be enough. Time is there for you to make something of it. Pockets of time are hiding in the corners, waiting to be found. Tools for accessing that time are at hand.

Time, it turns out, is on your side.

Ready to find out how? Here's how.

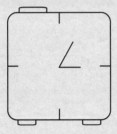

BEFORE WE
BEGIN

"The world is burning. I will have those content model updates ready by Thursday."

—EILEEN WEBB

Before we dive in to fixing our relationships with time, though, we need to take a close look at a couple of matters.

For one thing, we need to consider how economics and social-justice issues play into the discourse of everyone being too busy. It's never OK to just look at things from the default position of a dominant culture. We must figure out how we're going to stay woke.

Second, it would help to have some background. What historical forces in the 20th century led to 21st-century people feeling the way we do? Your grandparents had plenty of challenges of their own, but a constant feeling of near panic about time was probably not one of them. What happened?

Where we are and where we've been. Whose stories get told and whose have been left out. **Let's look at the cultural and historical factors at work here, before we start complaining about our in-boxes** (don't worry, we'll get to that, too).

"I think human societies tend to be problematic."

—TA-NEHISI COATES

The elephant in the room when it comes to talking about time—heck, if we're honest, when it comes to talking about just about anything—is privilege. Economic privilege and racial privilege and the way those two are inexorably intertwined.

Near the start of her book *Overwhelmed: Work, Love, and Play When No One Has the Time,* author Brigid Schulte, concerned that people think lack of time is some sort of yuppie problem, visits a group of working-poor immigrant families—folks working two or three jobs, living two or three families to an apartment, unable to afford childcare—and asks them whether they feel they don't have enough time in their day to do all the things they need to do. Every hand in the room goes up. She asks if they have time for leisure. Everyone just stares at her. "Maybe at church," one woman finally says, "or when I sleep."

This story neatly makes the point that, obviously, **lack of time is not just a middle-class problem.** Clearly a single mom working two low-paying jobs has a greater time problem on her hands than a married middle-class mom whose husband doesn't do the laundry. Lack of time in our modern era is an everyone problem. But, like most things, it's going to hit those with less privilege harder.

And while we may all be in the same boat of not having enough time, we're not all in the same boat when it comes to privilege. Ta-Nehisi Coates incisively details, in his essay "The Case for Reparations," how, throughout much of the 20th century, black people were shut out of one of the greatest wealth-building opportunities in American history: the middle-class home-buying boom—and how that fact continues to reverberate in racial economic disparities to this day. Race and economics are irreversibly tangled, and to deny the importance of either one to people's lived experience is to be willfully naïve.

And yet, so many people still assume that the audience interested in this topic is a bougie one. "Knowledge workers," "creatives," "freelancers," and "entrepreneurs"

are presumed to be the readers for a book such as the one you hold in your hands—and all those terms are stereotypically assumed to pertain to people who are variously privileged, relatively affluent, and probably white.

So, before we go further, let's stand for a moment in the reality that the 21st-century time crunch affects everyone, and that everyone is not the same. We live in a world of inequality and difference. And while many of the differences are beautiful, wonderful, and to be celebrated, others are the result of centuries of systemic oppression, of racism, of the rich getting richer and the poor getting poorer.

This book does not purport to be a universal panacea. What's in it may prove more useful to some individuals than to others. But let's never forget we all need help with these matters. Let's aim to make our conversations about time—its challenges and its possibilities—as open, equitable, and inclusive as possible.

"You're living life in fast forward. Your inbox is overflowing. Your days feel scattered in bits and fragments of what feels like Time Confetti. And maybe you think this is just the way life is."

—BRIGID SCHULTE

OK, so, really, what the heck is going on? *Why* does no one feel like they have enough time?

Turns out, like so many things, deep down **our lack of time is a feminist issue.** It comes down to work and the family, and the ways women's roles in those two arenas changed in the second half of the 20th century— and the ways our world did not change to keep up with them.

In *Overwhelmed,* Schulte goes on a journalistic deep dive to explain what the heck happened and how we got here. It emerges that the main thing that happened is that women entered the workforce. Not everyone remembers but, in the United States, we came very close to passing a federal universal childcare bill that would have addressed one of the biggest ramifications of that fact—what to do with the kids?—in a very direct manner. But at the last minute the bill was kiboshed by, of all people, Pat Buchanan. And families with two working parents (let alone a single working parent) have had to scramble ever since to figure out childcare, putting a huge strain not only on financial budgets, but also on time budgets.

The other thing that happened was that, although most women now work outside the home, we never really lost the notion that housework and children were mainly women's responsibilities. Schulte discovers that this largely stems from the relative prevalence of maternity leave in our society, and relative rarity of paternity leave. During maternity leave mothers become adept at caring for their babies. This expertise leads to the baby—and by extension the whole domestic sphere—becoming the mom's domain, even when the dad is around. This happens even to couples who were equitable in their division of domestic labor before they had kids—after children arrive couples tend to revert to traditional gender roles.

The solution to this conundrum is straightforward: paternity leave. Dads who spend time home alone with their babies become expert childcare-givers too, and a more equal division of child and household labor follows from that single fact. But paternity leave is rare.

Of course, it's not only moms, or only parents of children, or only straight couples, who feel the time crunch. The sweeping changes seen in recent decades in both work and technology have affected how everyone experiences time. Time is inevitably going to feel different when you're accessible via the small plastic rectangle in your pocket 24 hours a day.

Add to that the changing nature of our very concept of *being busy*—which has morphed from its original 18th-century meaning of being *happily occupied* to a sort of sick badge of honor meaning *I'm nearly drowning in work but at least that shows how important I am*—and you have a perfect storm. The confluence of modern-day factors could hardly have been better designed to make us all feel super short on time and pretty much miserable because of it.

LET'S EMPOWER OURSELVES

"We cannot retreat to the convenience of being overwhelmed."

—RUTH MESSINGER

It's so tempting to give up. To retreat, as Ruth Messinger eloquently put it, to the convenience of being overwhelmed.

Why does she call it "retreat"? And why "convenience"? There's nothing very safe or convenient about feeling overwhelmed, is there? Except insofar as once we've retreated, we don't have to fight anymore. Once we've declared we're officially overwhelmed we can, conveniently, stop trying.

Oh, all those big amazing but also kind of scary dreams you used to have—if you retreat, you no longer have to bother to pursue them. All the injustices in the world? Not your problem—you're too busy being busy. Nurturing empathic relationships with the people in your life? Who could expect you to do such a thing when you're so overwhelmed all the time?

Instead of writing yourself the depressing get-out-of-jail-free card of being overwhelmed, what if there was another way? What if we could get out from under the towering burden of our to-do lists? Not because there will ever be anything other than a plethora of things to do, but because we are going to change both our way of thinking about time and the practical tools we use to manage our time.

"I realized busyness had devoured my values."

—DAVID SBARRA

When we stop retreating into a helpless state of overwhelm, we reclaim our power. **The power to live our values.**

This isn't some vague self-help platitude. It is literally, practically, true. We may not have power over everything, but we do have power over this. Think about it—which would be more in accordance with your values: spending another ten minutes on email, or making time to call your congressperson? Doing another half hour of housework, or sitting down to draw with your kid?

This is not to say that the email and the housework—and the commuting and the cooking and all the rest of it—aren't important. Of course they're important and need to get done.

But they are not the boss of you. Your to-do list is not the boss of you. You are the boss of you. That's your power. And your values are how you decide what your boss (you, remember?) is going to have you do next.

"One must not think of life as an intrusion."

—SARAH RUHL

Being opposed to distraction is outdated. E. B. White said, "Creation is in part merely the business of foregoing the great and small distractions." And in some ways, hey, very good point there, E. B.

But in other ways, wow, what a privileged man-who-doesn't-have-to-take-care-of-the-kids thing to say. Recent women writers like Sarah Ruhl, Lydia Davis, and Rivka Galchen have made the interruptions and lack-of-time that come with modern life—and particularly modern motherhood—into so much creative fodder. They've made art out of it. And there's something phenomenally encouraging about that.

Davis's story "What You Learn about the Baby" is a masterwork of this idea of turning the interruptions into the work itself. Written in numerous tiny short sections, it contains, among other gems, these lines that epitomize the interruptions inherent in the parent's life: "You learn never to expect to finish anything. For example, the baby is staring at a red ball. You are cleaning some large radishes. The baby will begin to fuss when you have cleaned four and there are eight left to clean."

It's not just like, oh, look, Davis wrote about the scattered mind-set of parenthood. No. She turned that mind-set into the very fabric—both the form and the content—of an exquisitely beautiful piece of writing.

The idea that we have to wait for some ideal distraction-proof state to emerge in our brains or in our lives before we can properly work or create is absolutely poisonous and likely to result in never doing anything.

We are not going to solve our time problems by banishing distraction and mess. Not even if we choose a quite regimented schedule as one of our time–problem-solving techniques (which, as you will see, some people do and some do not). We are going to learn to work around and among and alongside of and, yes, even inside of the messiness to find the time we need.

"If you think about what you're here to do in life, the answer is probably not 'get really good at time management.'"

—JOCELYN K. GLEI

Glei, one of our foremost writers on productivity, adds: "Maybe getting overly obsessed about time management is really just a sleight of hand. One in which we spend all our energy focusing on a difficult task that we will inevitably never succeed at—in this case, controlling time—as a distraction from the more difficult task of confronting what we're really here on earth to do."

This is like that concept of retreating to the convenience of being overwhelmed turned on its head. Instead of giving in to the feeling of overwhelm, we'd be giving in to an endless spin cycle of reading productivity books and trying to get a handle on time when, of course, on a profound level, time is something outside our control.

But, on the other hand, if we're going to do the things "we're really here on earth to do," then, one way or another, we're going to have to make time to do them. Because we all know that **if we don't make time for them, they're not getting done.**

So this is where perspective comes in. We're going to need to balance the micro perspective—our desire to start using various practical tools to get our acts together—with the big picture perspective: a larger sweeping discovery and acceptance of the natures of time and work and, yes, joy.

That's why this book is short. So you can learn what you need to learn here, and then get out there and live.

"This is a wasting-time day, and I allot four hours of just doing nothing, so that the next day I can really focus."

—ISSA RAE

We can't always be only making time to be productive and get stuff done. Yes, yes, the stuff needs to get done. The little things and also the big, lifelong-dream things.

But we're also going to be carving out time to take walks. Time to get down on the floor and play with a child. Time to sit still and watch the world go by. Time just to be and not do much at all and see what happens.

If that kind of free-floating leisure sounds impossible and out of reach to you, well, that's why you're reading this book.

But if it sounds frivolous and wasteful and selfish to you, you've got another think coming.

We're going to talk a lot in this book about goals and tasks and accomplishments, yes. But at a certain point all of that only gets you so far. We don't want to turn you into some sort of task-accomplishing robot.

We want to bring more ease and joy into your life. **More creativity. More love. More delight.**

That's what happens when time is your friend and you stop being so insanely rushed all the time. You unfurl your wings and feel the sun on your back.

Not all the time. Maybe just now and then. It's really remarkable what a few small pockets of deliberate openness and leisure (which is different than just lying there at the end of the night scrolling on your phone or whatever) can do for your mind-set and even, for that matter, for your productivity the rest of the time.

"Let's go!"

—LIN-MANUEL MIRANDA

The modern-day challenge of no one having enough time to do the things they want to do is very real. No one is making this stuff up.

But the possibility of **using our smarts and tenacity to slide right through it and out the other side** is also entirely real.

We're going to ground ourselves in our power and our values; we're going to reframe our mind-sets; we're going to deploy a giant toolbox full of practical tools; and we're going to get time on our side.

Let's go.

THE THREE BIG CHANGES OF MIND-SET

"There is no list of rules. There is one rule. The rule is: There are no rules. Happiness comes from living as you need to, as you want to. As your inner voice tells you to. Happiness comes from being who you actually are instead of who you think you are supposed to be."

—SHONDA RHIMES

As long as you're walking around convinced you have to do all this stuff you think is expected of you, that your to-do list is the boss of you, that you don't have enough time and that can never change—well, frankly, you're screwed. It's never going to change. But that's **not the end of the story.**

"I don't focus on what I'm up against. I focus on my goals and I try to ignore the rest."

—VENUS WILLIAMS

There are two main ways you recalibrate your relationship with time.

What you probably think of as "productivity" or "time management"—practical tools, tips and tricks, work-arounds and life hacks—is the second way.

That stuff comes second because you can't get the most out of those sorts of strategies until you've done the first piece of work. Namely, adjusting your mind-set.

We have the ability to change things by changing the way we look at them.

Now, let's get crystal clear right away: This is most decidedly *not* some Horatio Alger bootstrapping, power-of-positive-thinking, law-of-attraction kind of nonsense we're talking about here. This is not some woo-woo self-help thing where you start vibrating at the frequency of money and suddenly find yourself rolling around in greenbacks like Scrooge McDuck; and if you're not rolling in dough (or, in our case, time), it's basically all your own fault for thinking the wrong thoughts.

Oh, *hell* no.

Like we said: The time problem is entirely real. It's societal. **It. Is. Not. Your. Fault.**

But that doesn't mean there aren't some basic changes you can make to how you think about it that will help you to find your way out of it. Will it ever be perfect? Nope. Will you still feel overwhelmed sometimes? Sure. You are a 21st-century human being, after all.

It's OK to feel overwhelmed sometimes. What's not OK is letting your brain trick you into feeling totally powerless when you in fact do have power. Believing there is nothing you can do when in fact there are things you can do.

We can tune up our ideas, spring clean the insides of our heads, tweak the settings on our minds. We can view the problem, and its possible solutions, differently. We can do this by thinking new thoughts about three things:

Prioritization

Procrastination

Pockets

"Whenever you hear or say, 'I don't have time'—it's a lie. Often a well-intentioned one, but whatever. We all have 24 hours in a day. Period. The accurate statement is, 'It's not a priority.'"

—ERIC BARKER

Barker's words are a wake-up call. The things you think you don't have time to do are the things you have deprioritized. **Getting completely lucid about what your top priorities are will radically alter how you experience time.**

A few priorities are preset for you. You have to do your work (be that paid work or unpaid work such as caregiving). You have to raise your kids if you have kids. You have to eat and sleep.

But you control *how* you do those things. You control whether you check work email at home. You control whether you bake for the bake sale. You control what time you go to bed and what time you get up.

And, once we've got the preloaded priorities out of the way, you have way more leeway when it comes to prioritizing the rest of the stuff in your life. How big a priority is housework—not for anyone else, but for you personally? Date night? Volunteering? Meditating? Working out? Taking baths? Protesting? Making art? Cooking? Reading?

If that list makes you want to shout "All of it! It's all a priority! It's all equally important," then you have not yet embraced the awesome power of triage.

The reason you might sit in the emergency room for hours with a broken arm is that you are not dying. And someone else is. Clearly, they need to treat the dying person before they treat your painful but not life-threatening broken bone. Your situation is important but it's not as urgent as the guy with the heart attack. That's triage.

You set the priorities for your life. You are in control. Not of everything. But of a whole heck of a lot of things. You're the doctor making the triage decisions. That's your power, right there. Claim it.

"There are an infinite number of things you could be doing. No matter what you work on, you're not working on everything else. So the question is not how to avoid procrastination, but how to procrastinate well."

—PAUL GRAHAM

Computer scientist Paul Graham's concept of *good procrastination* is nothing short of a revelation.

He goes on to explain: "There are three variants of procrastination, depending on what you do instead of working on something: You could work on (a) nothing, (b) something less important, or (c) something more important. That last type, I'd argue, is good procrastination . . . That's the sense in which the most impressive people I know are all procrastinators. They're type-C procrastinators: They put off working on small stuff to work on big stuff."

Are you getting this? **We can, and should, deploy procrastination as a tool of triage!**

When we put off that obligatory small thing (writing thank-you notes, say) to work on that important big thing (writing a novel, say), we are engaging in Graham's "good procrastination."

If prioritization is how we figure out what's really important to us, procrastination is how we figure out what we can let slide in order to make room for the important stuff.

It might be that, for you, the novel is actually the less important thing. Perhaps you're just working on that novel because you think it's what smart bookish people like you are supposed to do. Perhaps what you really want to do—what is for you bigger, more important—is writing those notes to your family and friends, nurturing those relationships, keeping up those important connections. Only you know for sure.

And you do know.

Graham wraps up his essay saying, "Let delight pull you instead of making a to-do list push you . . . and you'll leave the right things undone." When we make *delight* one of our metrics for choosing which tasks to prioritize and which to procrastinate, things suddenly get a whole lot clearer.

"Change will not come . . . if we wait for some other time."

—BARACK OBAMA

Let's be real.

It's not going to be all delight all the time.

You need clean socks, so you need to do laundry. Probably not too much delight there (unless you count smooshing your face down into the just-out-of-the-dryer clean clothes and letting their warmth envelop you—and it's strongly recommended that you indeed do count that).

As much as we'd all love to chase joy and urgency all day long, the reality is that most of the hours in the day are already spoken for. In fact, right now, it probably feels like *all* the hours are spoken for, and then some. Workers gotta work. Sleepers gotta sleep. Parents gotta parent. And so on and so forth.

But the remarkable thing you're going to discover is **the immense power of locating and dedicating small pockets of time** in your day, week, month, or year for the things you really want to be doing. Sometimes they'll be truly tiny, sometimes a bit bigger.

It is truly astonishing to observe how much can be accomplished (even if that "much" is intentionally actually sort of nothing—like people-watching or meditation) in relatively brief pockets of time carved out regularly.

Much of the rest of this book is concerned with exactly how to do that carving out in your own life. But before you go on to read about *how* to do it, you have to believe that you *can* do it. That it is possible. That this magical tool with the silly name (be honest now: Who among you didn't raise an eyebrow back on page 33 when the list of the three big mind-set game changers ended with the word "Pockets"?) is going to fundamentally alter your reality.

A lofty claim? Oh yeah. You'll soon see why.

ALL THE
STUFF WE NEED
TO DO

"The world needs our immediate presence."

—LOUISE PENNY, PARAPHRASING MIGUEL CERVANTES

Somehow, we all have to show up. Whether it's the world that's demanding our presence or our own selves, we've all got to find a way to show the hell up in our lives.

Everyone reinvents this wheel for themselves. No two people are handling this time mess in exactly the same way. People are figuring out the strategies that work best for them.

What allows folks to make time for the things that matter to them? It can seem like others are balancing everything effortlessly. They're not. A lot of thought and hard work are going into making things work.

By examining how a wide range of regular, everyday people make time—for their work, families, relationships, practicalities, creativity, activism, and selves—we can start sorting out which of their strategies might work for us and, just as importantly, which might not. What to use and what to discard.

People do all kinds of stuff. Let's see what we discover.

"What do people do all day?"

—RICHARD SCARRY

Oh, work. Sometimes it feels like it takes up all our time, just by itself.

And, in some ways, we have no choice about it. After all, we have to earn a living. But in fact, we do have a degree of agency. We can think about how we *organize* our working lives.

While things like flexible schedules or remote work are not available to everyone, it can nevertheless be useful to examine some variations to the typical workday. Not only might we find something we could perhaps try, but, also, **looking at others' creative solutions can inspire wholly new ideas about what our own work might be and how we might do it.**

Here are six people who work in somewhat unconventional ways, whose normal day-to-day experiences challenge what we think a work day can look like. You'll know right away which of these ideas are (or are not) exciting to you. Use that knowledge.

Tiffanie, an artist, often works from late evening until the wee hours of the morning. She says, "As many times as I've tried to shift my schedule back to the 'normal' circadian rhythm enjoyed by my family and friends, I find I cannot resist the temptation of working at night. Nighttime (or 'second shift,' as we call it in our house) is when I am guaranteed no one is going to disrupt my work for five or six hours. I can become as absorbed as I need to be." Likewise, people who'd dislike these sorts of almost-all-nighters sometimes get similar results by rising as early as four in the morning.

Erin, a production coordinator, works in an office, but works from home each Friday. Working remotely means she can slow down, focus, and look at the big picture. "Mondays through Thursdays my thoughts are racing from one task to another," she says. "I am running from one meeting to another—sometimes literally! By Friday I am usually exhausted and behind. Working from home gives me time to concentrate on individual responsibilities (compared to the more collaborative or supportive work I tend to do in the office) and provides a space for uninterrupted, deliberate thought."

Shweta, a writer, divides her time between being a full-time parent to her two young daughters and a freelance journalist. "For me," she says, "taking work on a project-by-project basis is the best scenario while caring for my children while they're still small. It's important for me to keep up my skills and to have some presence in my industry. Finding good childcare is a must, as is maximizing my writing hours sans baby by having a game plan before I sit down to work." For some, freelance work is a full-time career, but it can also form a part-time option for those with other things on their plates.

Kate is a literary agent who works from a home office. She points out that "working from home means I can structure my day not only around my job, but also around my personal life and my mood. The two hours per day I used to spend commuting now go toward exercise, cooking dinner for my family, running errands so they don't consume our weekend, and spending time with my kids. Not commuting also means I have more time each day to focus on the work—that allows me to work longer, more efficient days Monday through Thursday and take Fridays off to spend with my youngest daughter."

Lisa C., an illustrator, has found that sometimes you need to say no to projects, even when technically you could cram them into your schedule. She notes that "when you say yes to too many projects at once, you quickly use up your reserves of creative energy and the freshness and quality of your work deteriorates." This is true not only for freelancers, who must pick their projects one at a time, but also for folks with more conventional 9-to-5s: The autonomy to choose what we are and are not going to work on is one of the greatest forms of independence we can work toward in our careers.

Bryant is an activist, author, and chef. At any given time, he's doing multiple gigs—working with a museum, traveling for public speaking, and tackling side projects. But what makes the biggest difference is whether he's writing a cookbook. "My work-family balance is like a seesaw," he says. When not on deadline, "I'm the one who manages our daughters' lives for the most part." He handles their activities, shopping, school runs, and so forth. "But when I have a looming book deadline, things shift dramatically. I miss family dinners, weekends, holidays. But the payoff is that after my book is done I go back to spending lots of my time with the family."

"Women can have it all. Yeah, stop saying that. You act like *all* is good. *All* does not mean good. You've never left an all-you-can-eat buffet and thought, I feel really good about myself. That crab and pudding is sitting really well together."

—MICHELLE WOLF

Family is big and messy, full of challenges and full of love. **Family sucks up our time maybe even more than work—and its rewards are infinitely greater.**

Family isn't just motherhood anymore (if it ever was). It's dads and grandparents, aging parents and relatives abroad, stay-at-home parents and stepchildren. A web of connections. Who we care for and how.

Kristen W. E. is a full-time parent. Her two kids have special needs and, because of this, "we have more appointments, advocating, and bureaucracy to deal with than your average family. We also need to be with our kids more and find more professional care for them, which limits our options for things like afterschool care." Contrary to sexist fantasies about "housewives" with wide-open days, time-management is key: "Family time is essential: We eat together, play together, do chores together. But we also have clear downtime, adult-only time, one-on-one time with each kid, and time to discuss parenting matters. We build in safeguards, like solo getaways, to give me emotional support."

Christina's father was from Iran, where intergenerational living is more common. "When I was pregnant," she relates, "my wife and I moved in with my mom. My dad had died, and my mom was living in a big house by herself. When our baby needed to be held, we had another set of hands. Now, our children are older, and they love living with Nana. And for my mother, our living arrangement allows her not to have to cook anymore. My wife does nearly all the cooking and shopping—my mom does art projects with the kids while she cooks. We all have more of the life that we want."

Ana is a law student in California. Her family lives in Puerto Rico. With the time difference, she used to struggle to find times to call them. Then she started walking to work and calling her family as she walked. She rotates calls each day between her mother (with whom she's healed a previously strained relationship), her father (who now "gets" his daughter better than he ever did before), and her grandmother (who has since had a stroke; it's harder to understand her words now, but the emotional meaning is clear as ever). "Though I've never lived further away, I've never felt closer to my family than I do now."

Bruno is a stay-at-home dad. He says the reversal from a traditional gender role is "the most difficult—but also the most refreshing—part." He elaborates, "Being a full-time parent is not something most men were ever taught to imagine for ourselves. Yet the joy of being there for my kids is the best experience I've ever had. It's an ongoing, exhilarating, frustrating, and exhausting life experience. In the end, my kids have become my life's work." As with many stories of how families manage their time, it's the unexpected way of doing things—the surprise we didn't see coming—that turns out to work best for a particular family.

Joel is a journalist. When his wife finished maternity leave, he took paternity leave to stay home with his infant daughter. "I had never taken care of a baby before my daughter was born," he relates. "Taking the months off to be with her at the beginning of her life seemed critical to our mutual understanding. I have no doubt that I am a better parent, husband, and person for that time. And, call me naïve, but I also feel certain that when she is a teenager in grave doubt about her father's advice, somewhere deep inside she will understand it comes from love, rooted in those early days together."

Jen, who had three daughters, married a man with two daughters and a son. *Brady Bunch* jokes aside, what's it like with six kids? "Honestly, our life is chaos. While our children spend the majority of their time with us, we also share them between two other homes—coupled with their busy afterschool commitments, our schedule is in constant flux. What I have learned is to not let the unpredictability drive me crazy. It is what it is. And it's so important to prioritize our downtime together. We always, always, always make time for sit-down family dinner. Even if that means instant ramen, store-bought rotisserie chicken, and frozen peas!"

"I didn't fall in love, I rose in it."

—TONI MORRISON

There's a lot of talk about how much we work. About balancing careers with family. About making time for creativity or self-care or other things that matter to the individual.

But there's not really much dialog about how to make time for our romantic relationships. How to prioritize our connection with **the one person we actually liked well enough to go ahead and commit ourselves to.**

Especially amid the chaos of childrearing, the person who helped you become a parent in the first place is often the one with the second-least amount of time allocated to them (the first-least being, almost certainly, yourself—but we'll get to that in a bit).

This fact is used, again and again, to comedic effect in the movies, usually at the woman's expense (think *Knocked Up*), although not always (think *Date Night*). But punchlines and stereotypes aside, and with or without kids in the picture, this is a real thing. A serious thing.

How do we make time for love? Could there be a better question?

Benjamin, who works for a natural grocery chain, is "a big fan of date night." He elaborates: "We schedule the babysitter to show up at 5:30 every other Friday whether we have plans or not. Occasionally, we're tired and don't even want to go out. Do we cancel date night? Hell no! We've had dates where we just stayed in, ordered takeout, and watched a movie. Time alone together is the oxygen for our relationship." He goes on, "We also do another thing that dovetails with this—on Tuesday nights my wife is 'off' and I get Thursdays 'off.'" They essentially give each other the gift of time.

Matthew, a children's book author, works with his wife, who is an illustrator. "Creatively collaborating with someone who also sleeps in the same bed at night," he says, "is great because we're always available to each other, able to nuance an idea in the course of a walk around the park or a three-hour drive to New York City. We can be more constant and leisurely about our collaboration." On the other hand, "it's awful because we're always available to each other, unable to leave a problem at the office or pretend we never got that email. Unaddressed work issues can become festering life issues. But the benefits dwarf the downsides."

Deanne and her husband lived apart 12 days out of 14 for a year—she in their home city, he four hours away where he was in school to become a professional woodworker. "In the year we lived apart," she shares, "we found ways to be together in slices of time we usually wasted. We had a standing Facetime date in the morning while getting ready and in the evenings just before sleep. We were able to spend about an hour 'together' each day without giving up any of the time we needed for our creative pursuits, seeing friends and family, and dealing with everyday tasks that make up life."

Andrea, who lived in Baltimore, fell in love with a man who lived in Sweden. "The blessing and the burden of a long-distance relationship is the long distance," she opines. "I met my husband while he was visiting Washington, DC, just days before his return home. We had a mere 48 hours to hang out. Then we spent the next few weeks, before my first visit to Stockholm, on the phone chatting away getting to know one another. Although the distance impacted our courtship in that we weren't able to physically date, I appreciated our long conversations about nothing and everything. It was so different from anything I'd experienced before."

Allison and her wife run a small business together and are parents of a child with special needs. She talks about the importance of partners looking out for one another, each taking things on so the other can have a break. "I feel like one of us is always stepping up while the other is stepping back," she says. "Allowing each other to travel is the biggest and best way we do this. I hold down the fort while she attends conferences, and she stays home so I can go to writing retreats in the redwoods." Couples don't nurture relationships only by being together, but also by supporting one another.

Wynn and his husband both work in tech. With two busy careers they've realized one of the best things they can do for their relationship is to prioritize making the time to take trips together. He explains: "Travel is like a gift for ourselves that keeps on giving. First, it's a beacon on our calendars; then, it's an adventure we're sharing, and it ends up being a memory we have forever. What's better than that?" It's an amazing thought that time spent with a loved one—whether traveling or at home—counts triple: in anticipation, in memory, and in the moment.

"You are not obligated to complete the work, but neither are you free to abandon it."

—RAMI SHAPIRO

The laundry. The taxes. The groceries. Taking the dog to the vet. Mowing the lawn. Making dentist appointments. Making dinner. Packing lunches. Vacuuming. Paying bills. Ordering a new alarm clock with overnight shipping because the old one broke. Getting the oil changed. Going to the drugstore. On and on and on.

You could fill a whole book with the stuff we need to get done. **It's not glamorous or fun, but it has to happen if our lives are to run smoothly.**

And it drives us bananas. In those spiraling moments of panic—and we've all had them—over too much to do and not enough time to do it, it's the errands, house-work, and paperwork that seem to crush us.

How the hell do people get all this stuff done? we want to shout. How does anyone?

Because Lisa A. is self-employed and her husband works a corporate job, she's the one who handles things like sick kids, taking the car in, or waiting around for repair people. She points out that, by freeing him up from these practical tasks, she effectively *sponsors* his career. She elaborates, "Sponsorship is the role a working partner plays in the advancement of their mate's career. When both partners work and one clocks out during normal work hours to tend to their shared responsibilities, the sponsored partner's workday remains uninterrupted. Naming this often-unintentional effect of one partner's flexibility on the other's work life is important when striving toward partner equality."

Jenn and her husband both work full time. "In a home with two breadwinners, all the housework still needs to be done. I've had to come to terms with the fact that I really can't do it all. But I can make choices. I can choose do to things I enjoy (like cooking or packing my daughter's lunch) and outsource things I don't: going to the store, laundry, cleaning. Compared to the cost of cutting back on work, services like grocery delivery, wash-and-fold, and housecleaning are remarkably affordable." Such buying of time is not affordable for everyone. But if you do have the money, don't feel guilty about choosing to spend it this way.

Mirabelle lives with three roommates in a large house, so there's a lot to clean and plenty of variables—how often each space needs cleaning, how many people are needed to clean it, and so forth. Rather than arguing about whose turn it is to do what, the four women have concocted a clever system: "We created a spreadsheet on a whiteboard, with people on the y axis, chores on the x axis, and dates in the cells. When you complete a task, you simply erase the date and write in the next date when that task will fall to you. It keeps us accountable and the house clean!"

Alan and his wife are working parents of preschool-age twins. "Basically," he says, "every minute of our life is allocated. My wife does mornings, I do evenings. I loathe mornings, but she goes to bed by 8:30ish, so she wakes up refreshed and ready to go. I'm a night owl and stay up late doing stuff like making lunches and taking care of paperwork. I wake up 15 minutes before I leave the house, work through lunch, and leave work by 4:00 to pick up the kids by 5:30ish. Make dinner, eat, put the kids in the bath and do dishes while they splash around. Put them to bed. Repeat."

Bill, a middle school teacher, talks about men and women being equal partners in managing the home. "It's more about equity than equality: Not every task has to be split down the middle, but the overall amount of stuff we're each handling should feel equal and fair to both of us. Take cooking dinner—we used to alternate weeks for who cooked. But over time we realized, I really enjoy cooking as a way to relax after work, and my wife does not. So now I cook most nights while she helps our daughter with homework (which, after teaching all day, is the last thing I want do when I get home)."

Tiffany, a creative coach and podcast host, runs her business from her home. So how do you divide your housework from your work-work when both reside inside the same physical space? Tiffany says, "My biggest success in keeping my work and home life separate is to *literally keep things separate.* I set working hours for myself where I don't try to pay bills or fold clothes or clean the kitchen. I physically separate my workspace as much as possible—bonus points if you have a door you can close!—both to keep the home out of the office and to keep the office out of the rest of the home."

"The most regretful people on earth are those who felt the call to creative work, who felt their own creative power restive and uprising, and gave to it neither power nor time."

—**MARY OLIVER**

If, at our most time-addled, housework is the monster that looms over us, creativity is the ghost that sits in the corner and weeps.

Everyone is creative. We know creative expression is good for us. We want to find time for creativity, but we struggle to do so. Or we don't make it happen and then feel bad.

Creativity doesn't have to involve art supplies. For some people it's music. For some it's craft. For some it's a hobby. For some a life's work. All have something to teach us.

Vanessa, a librarian, does needlework. She relates, "Embroidery is the tangible way I connect to the women who made my life possible. I'm literally continuing the traditions of my foremothers—all the women in my family did needlework of one kind or another. And it calms me—it feels akin to meditation. I'm hyper-focused while also letting my mind wander freely. Plus, I can take it anywhere and do it anytime. Jury duty, plane flights, conferences, long waits in the doctor's office—I look forward to things most people dread because they afford me time to do my favorite thing." Oh, the magical power of finding pockets of time!

Rachael (an art director) and two friends started a ladies' drawing night. "It helped me turn a corner with my art-making practice as a new mom," she remembers, "because it combined desperately needed social time and desperately needed creative time. And, because I wanted to be prepared for those evenings, I started making studies for future drawings on subway rides. I realized I could break down my creative process into three-minute segments. Literally, three minutes. Then, that practice expanded and I started writing, on my phone, on the subway, in small increments as well. I

wrote two (now published!) children's books that way."
Like Vanessa, Rachael found a use for previously dead
pockets of time.

Rae is a ceramicist. But she has a morning routine based
on an entirely different form of creativity. Before starting
work each day, she practices music. "I think of playing
the piano as a form of brain yoga, and part of my daily
exercise regime. The mental demands of piano playing
are rigorous, but at the same time it quickly transports
me to a zone that allows me to relax and to think
creatively." Accessing that creative part of the brain is
of course vital for someone who will spend the day
doing creative work. But creative thinking can be equally
important for those with other types of jobs.

Katharine quit her job as an accountant to start a business
that provides artists' residencies and workshops. She says,
"I found that once I quit my (soul-sucking, non-creative)
job, and started my arts-based business, my creativity—
impulses, insights, inspiration, energy—expanded
exponentially. This was true both relating directly to my
business and to my own practice as a maker and artist.
Sometimes being a creative entrepreneur feels like a
runaway train, but it always feels like the right one."

Creativity doesn't have to be relegated to a hobby or side hustle. For some, quitting the day job and making the creative life the full-time job is the perfect move.

On the other hand, having a day job can sometimes be energizing. Rebecca, an actress, writer, and musician, works for a digital events company. "My day job is an anchor structure for my creative work. I've had periods where entire days stretched out before me, and the mental energy needed to make the most of those days was sapping." She does creative work for half an hour first thing in the morning, during a 20-minute break in the afternoon, and on planes and trains during work trips, as well as in evenings and on weekends. "There's a delight in finding pockets of time for creativity that might otherwise go to social media spacing out."

Just like a day job can, a side-hustle may also be a surprising creative catalyst. For several years, Brian, a writer, artist, and art director, drove for a ride-hailing company a few nights a week. Even more than being an extra source of income, "it was a way to clear my head. San Francisco is beautiful at night. The roads are empty and you meet a lot of characters. I kept a sketchbook in the car. In the short breaks between fares, I wrote notes about each ride, and I drew pictures." Creative work and paid work are not as far apart as we think—anything that works to shake up your routine can inspire.

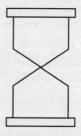

"Activism is the rent I pay for living on the planet."

—ALICE WALKER

Many more of us are activists now than were just a few years ago. The world is changing. In some ways drastically for the worse and in some glimmering ways for the better. **The ways things are getting worse require us to fight. And the ways things are getting better are because we are fighting.**

In addition to being a humanity-scale endeavor of critical importance, activism has—let's be real here—become yet another demand clamoring for the precious few hours we have "free" each day. How to make time to help save the world?

Well, for one thing, how can we not? Turning our backs would be gross negligence. But we also can't keep banging our heads against a wall over and over again without respite. That way lies burnout and disaffection.

People are figuring this stuff out. Finding means of support. Ways of fitting the desperate measures that desperate times call for into their everyday laundry-and-email-and-calling-mom lives.

Kathy and a few of her friends formed an activism support group. What started as a private Facebook group for sharing articles and venting has evolved into a real force for action: "Now we're all on the board of our regional ACLU chapter, and have joined up with people outside our usual circle—lawyers and those seasoned in political engagement—to increase our network and impact." Kathy continues: "Activism is difficult work. It requires stamina and persistence when the wins are few and the challenges plentiful. Having a group keeps us account-able, gives us energy, and frankly makes it more fun, which is necessary for the long haul."

Educator and artist Lisa S. started Artists Take Action— an Instagram-based auction. Each month, nine artists donate work, with money going straight to charity. "Time is not something I have a lot of. But community is. A lot of artists may not have a lot of money to donate, but we all have art we can give away! I support protesting or phone-banking, but those things don't fit into my life very well. This fits because I can do it in stolen moments between taking care of other things. The key is to play to your strengths. What are you good at? Small things can and do matter."

Tess, a baker, has called her senate and congressional lawmakers' offices every day for eighteen months and has no plans of stopping anytime soon. She elaborates: "It's an amazing way to stay politically involved in just three minutes a day. Seriously, three minutes! I have all my representatives' office numbers in my contacts. Sometimes I'll write myself a little script. And I call every evening after office hours so I can just leave messages." Again, small pockets of time add up. And it's reassuring to hear you don't necessarily have to talk to a person. "Decide what's important to you and have your voice heard!"

Sheila, a photographer, takes pictures at Black Lives Matter protests. "I consider myself an observer," she says. "My activism is storytelling, using the medium of photography as a form of art activism. I'm giving voice to the unheard. When I'm on the ground at a protest I'm so focused on what's happening that I lose myself in capturing the images. I create images from the emotions that are expressed by people while they are protesting—I've seen the sadness, hurt, fear, anger, and love in the community. It's about me as an African American; we need to tell our own narratives." She uses her unique skill set to politically engage.

Kristen H. organizes bake sales at her office to fundraise for victims of natural disasters. "I'm inspired by Dr.

Martin Luther King Jr.," she explains. "In a speech at Oberlin, he said, 'All mankind is tied together . . . in a single garment of destiny,' and also, 'The time is always right to do right.' Those words are a call to action: to not sit idly by when we see someone in need. No matter how busy we are, we can find the time to make a difference." Finding the core of our engagement, the words or philosophy that inspires our actions, can be a touchtone of support we return to again and again.

Maurice describes himself as essentially having "three full-time jobs: I'm a dad, a professional designer, and the executive director of a nonprofit." By taking on what amounts to a second, unpaid, career, running an organization to help students of color enter the field of design, he has made himself a very busy man. He elaborates: "Budgeting time should be a decision that makes your life, your existence on earth, meaningful and full of joy first. When days get full, the things that drive my commitments are the benefits of my investment of time—a person helped, time with family, prayer, etc.—nothing that results in something tangible in return."

"These are the three marriages of work, self, and other."

—DAVID WHYTE

In his book *The Three Marriages,* David Whyte proposes that we are married. Not only married in the obvious way, to our spouses, but also married to our work and, most radical notion of all, married to our own selves.

While Whyte's focus on spouses—to the seeming exclusion, or at least back-seating, of children, friends, siblings, nieces and nephews, parents—may seem a tad myopic, his essential and extremely valid point remains: **When we leave *self* out of the equation we're leaving out an essential piece.**

We ignore our marriage to our own sweet selves—to our emotional and spiritual and mental and physical health—at our peril. We know this. But, yet again, it's a matter of *who has the time?*

The answer, it turns out, is *lots of people*. Lots of people make the time to do the things they need to do to take care of themselves. To nurture their marriages with themselves. And you can too.

Maggi, a psychology student, is clear about the importance of going to therapy. "I never regret making time for talk therapy. I do regret the time I spent wanting things to change while doing nothing to get myself there—but that regret in itself is a waste of time." She also makes time to talk about it: "'Coming out' as someone who struggles with my mental health has been the best thing I've ever done for myself. I don't hide the fact that it is a lot of work for me to be a human existing in the world. I hope talking openly about it contributes to destigmatizing mental illness."

Two afternoons a week, Casey, an elementary school teacher, attends a boot-camp–style exercise class at a local park. She takes her two children with her—they play or do homework while she works out. Fitness has "become something I need to do. It makes me feel more confident. I can see the progress I've made and want to get stronger and faster." After class she hurries home to cook dinner—not out of obligation but because she enjoys it, "I find the time to cook because I've always liked doing it. With both the cooking and the working out, there's the added bonus of modeling that behavior to my kids."

But self-care doesn't have to be all going to therapy and working out, either. Kelly, a vice president at a manufacturing company, works on vintage cars. "I've always been interested in cars," he says, "but the older cars have more soul. I see a '69 Mustang Fastback and I'm vividly transported back to the driver's seat of my first car. When you're passionate about something, you make the time. You set goals to complete your 'must do's' so you can work on your 'want to's.'" He adds, "It's important for couples to understand and be supportive of each other's pursuits. In this way, I consider myself a very lucky man."

Ginee, a publishing executive, has been practicing transcendental meditation for two decades. "I do it twice a day, as soon as I wake up and again in the evening, about 30 minutes each session. The second session is harder to fit in, but I find even 15 minutes on the train ride home is helpful. I started when I was going through an extremely stressful time at work. Meditating allowed me to let go of outcomes in a way that had been impossible before. I think it's because regular practice gets you to a place of deep rest every day. It's more than worth the hour in my day."

Kim is an avid yoga practitioner. "I make time for yoga because it helps me feel grounded. I may have a growing list of to-dos, but when I'm doing yoga, I'm fully present in the here and now. In the end, I always feel better and happier." For some people, the firm structure of a class that happens at a particular time, or an unbreakable personal routine, is the way to go. But for others, like Kim, a more organic approach to scheduling time for ourselves works better: "I usually try to carve out 15 to 45 minutes in the morning or evening, a few times a week, using free online classes."

Stephen, who works in online marketing, bakes bread weekly. "Without planning for it to become a 'thing,' baking snuck into my life," he explains. It's not just about making the time for this creative practice, but why: "Baking bread is a matter of life and death. If I don't take the time to feed the sourdough starter, that colony of yeast in the mason jar in my fridge will die. And, for me, baking has been an act of soul preservation. Somewhere along the way, repeating this process has taught me that I'm pretty darn good at baking, and, more importantly, I'm really good at being me."

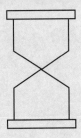

THE PROS AND CONS OF PRODUCTIVITY THINKING

"That whole thing about multitasking? That's a joke for me. When I try to do that, I don't do anything well."

—OPRAH WINFREY

There's no doubt that productivity as such—all the calendaring and life-hacking and multitasking and establishing of routines and counting of minutes—**has both its good and its bad sides.**

Without this type of thinking to help us, we can all too often find our relationship to time getting totally screwed up and making us miserable.

But when we deploy productivity-style thinking, we run the all-too-real risk of piling more on, stressing ourselves out, running like hamsters in our wheels, and all for what?

Before we go any further down the productivity path, let's pause and carefully consider the good, the bad, and the ugly of these types of approaches.

"That void interval which passes for him so slowly . . . that same interval, perhaps, teems with events, and pants with hurry for his friends."

—CHARLOTTE BRONTË

Productivity thinking has its problems. And we'll talk about those in just a moment. But, nevertheless, we need it. It's really the only tool that early 21st-century people have fashioned so far to address the unique time challenges of living in our particular historical moment.

Nineteenth-century people, for instance, had a different time problem. Or at least ones of certain social classes did. If you were upper class and didn't work at all, or if you were middle class and worked during the day and then came home to your candlelit home to spend each long evening, you had the problem of *too much* time.

Thus, the invention of the Victorian novel. Those long books full of long sentences were perfect for filling the long hours that stretched before you when you had servants to do all the housework; no TV and no social media and no gym; relatively little responsibility for raising your own children; and quite possibly a spouse whom you had little or no interest in hanging out with.

We have to stop thinking of productivity as a buzzword and start thinking of it as an occasion for joyfully solving one of the problems of our age. It must become our Victorian novel.

Something which runs the risk of being deeply boring must become something lighthearted and magical: **the thing that clears room in our lives for delight.**

"Just make sure you really want all those things you're working so hard to maintain."

—TIFFANY HAN

Like a scrumptious cupcake, the productivity promise is nearly irresistible. How sweet would it be to just master some set of tips and—poof!—all your time problems disappear?

The first bite is delicious. You learn something new. Find a hack for your routine. Uncover an erroneous way you've been thinking. Awesome.

So, you eat your cupcake, and you are happy. Want a second one? You might. Cupcakes are tasty. Yum. How about a third? A fourth? At what point do you start to feel ill?

If all you're learning is how to cram more and more things into your life, eventually it's going to be too much. Any system that doesn't invite you to take some things *out* of your life, to make room for the things you want to let *in*, is not working in your best interest.

"Having a system results in habitual rather sporadic creativity."

—SRINIVAS RAO

Yes, we need to embrace productivity and time-management techniques. A change of mind-set alone won't get us there. We need practical tools.

And we have to be realistic about what these tools are meant to do. **Some tools help us build and some tools help us prune.** Some tools assemble and some cut. We're going to be adding some things into our lives and taking some other things out, as well as moving stuff around.

Rather than a deluge of sweet promises we're going to assemble a toolbox full of utensils to choose from. A place where, bearing our priorities in mind, we can reach down and pick up what we need and deploy it to shape our realities to work the way we need them to work.

TIPS, TRICKS,
AND LIFE HACKS

"Are you really going to be upset because you're really busy? Some people are not busy and are praying that they could be as busy as you are."

—JANELLE MONÁE

Here come the productivity-minded tips and tricks. The brass tacks of time management that can help you reclaim your time. All are interdependent with a change of mind-set.

As you read about these strategies, **imagine yourself deploying them.** Think about which might fit you and which might not—which might solve your particular problem, and which are just not your cup of tea.

But remember, if you're tempted to think "that sounds great, but *I* couldn't pull it off," pause and reconsider. Empowering yourself to pull it off might be exactly what you need.

"Make it a recurring appointment in your calendar and plan on sticking to it."

—ANAHAD O'CONNOR

Perhaps the number-one thing we can do to make time for a particular activity is to put it on our calendar. It doesn't matter if we're talking about making time to jog or to draw or to volunteer or to work on a long-term project at our job. Whatever that priority of ours may be that we find ourselves struggling to make time for in our days, this is quite likely the solution.

Look hard at your calendar and figure out the best time to do the thing. Should you focus on that work project for an hour first thing when you start work in the morning a couple of days a week, *before* you check email? (Much more about email starting on page 85.) Can you make time for exercise before work, or after? Is there a particular evening of the week you could block out for that personal creative project? A recurring weekend slot when you could fit in time for that family activity or social justice cause?

A few tips to really make this work:

Once it's on your calendar, you have to believe it. The same way you'd believe a calendar appointment that popped up for a dentist appointment or a meeting with your boss. Things on your calendar are real and you're really going to do them on the day and at the time the calendar says you are.

And, remember, to find these pockets of time you previously didn't know existed, you're going to have to use your prioritization skills and make use of some of that good kind of procrastination. What can you move or scrunch or let go of entirely in order to make time for these higher-priority things?

Is that half hour you collapse on the sofa when you get home with your phone and a beer essential self-care time? Or could that time be better used for something else? Only you know the answer to that question, and you only really know it if you're willing to be brutally honest with yourself.

"So many people trip in front of them because they're looking over there or up ahead."

—KAMALA HARRIS

A to-do list that floats in its own isolated bubble—be that bubble a notebook or an app or something else— just sitting there waiting for you to come and choose a task whenever you have a moment to spare, is not only oppressive (who wants to be followed around by a bubble full of things-you-really-ought-to-be-doing all the time?), it's also not terribly effective.

After all, much of the time you'll be called upon to do things other than what's on the list. This is how you can have something like "make optometrist appointment" or "change 401(k) allocations" sit on your to-do list for liter- ally years. There was always something more important. It was never that thing's turn.

Plus, every time you *do* have time to do something from the list, you end up wasting precious time looking up ahead—for example, going over the list and figuring out which of the various things on it you ought to do.

Many of the most productive people avoid this pitfall by hybridizing their to-do list and their calendar.

This can be done in any number of ways:

- Perhaps you take ten minutes each morning to insert to-do list items, as appointments, into all the open slots in your calendar for that day.

- Perhaps each time you add an item to your to-do list you assign it a do-date rather than a due-date (that is, the date you actually plan to do it, and when you foresee having enough time to do it, as opposed to the date it's due).

- Maybe you jot down calendar notations for your evenings—which night you'll do laundry, which night you'll work on your taxes, which night you know you'll just want to chill.

- Maybe you even go so far as to get rid of your to-do list altogether—every task that arises going immediately onto the calendar instead. This works best with electronic rather than paper calendars, since inevitably things end up needing to get moved around.

Whatever particular system you employ, the underlying win is the same. You're weaving the stuff you need to do and the time you have to do it in into a cohesive whole in your mind. Tasks and time become teammates working together rather than opposing teams duking it out in the arena of your brain.

"People live too much of their lives on email."

—TRACY MORGAN

Oh, email. If you work in an office or an otherwise correspondence-heavy industry, chances are you regularly (or always) feel like you're drowning in your in-box.

In her book *Unsubscribe: How to Kill Email Anxiety, Avoid Distractions, and Get Real Work Done,* Jocelyn K. Glei tackles our collective problems with email—from our obsession with checking our in-boxes to the elusive etiquette of writing good messages. Perhaps most valuable of all are her insights into crafting a daily email routine.

Numerous experts agree these strategies are effective. Numerous happy workers have discovered their merits. Yet, until you try them, such ideas sound nearly impossible. You'll read what comes next and think, "Oh, sure, that's great for someone else, but I could never do it." But the thing is you can. **You *can* put reasonable limits on email and use the time you gain back for other, more important work.** You really, really can. Three tools, drawn from Glei's research, show us how:

1. *Don't do email first.* Glei suggests spending the first hour of your day on "a task that advances your meaningful work goals." Make it one of those calendar appointments from page 80. Set your email program to open not to your in-box but to your calendar. So the first thing you see when you sit down to work will be that appointment telling you to do that important work now.

2. *Corral email into two or three blocks of time per day*—each block a half hour (or at most an hour) long. Put the email blocks on your calendar as appointments and, once again, treat those appointments as commitments. Start working through your in-box when the appointment time starts, and stop when it ends.

3. *Don't have your in-box open* on your desktop while you're working on other things. Either switch it to show your calendar or shut the program down entirely.

Another useful thing is to *decide on your own personal nonresponse rate.* Articulating to yourself, "Of the emails I receive that could warrant a response, I respond to 95 percent" (or 90 percent or 80 percent or whatever feels right) will be liberating. As author Mark McGuinness puts it: "It's better to disappoint a few people over small things than to surrender your dreams for an empty in-box."

"The single most important change you can make in your working habits is to switch to creative work first, reactive work second."

—MARK MCGUINNESS

OK, so if we're not doing email first, what exactly are we doing first?

McGuinness writes that "creative work first, reactive work second" means "blocking off a large chunk of time every day for creative work on your own priorities, with the phone and email off. I used to be a frustrated writer. Making this switch turned me into a productive writer. Now, I start the working day with several hours of writing. I never schedule meetings in the morning if I can avoid it. So whatever else happens I get my important work done."

He is a writer so the creative work he needs to do first is, not surprisingly, writing.

But this doesn't apply only to those who work in creative fields. Just like a writer should write first and email later, an executive ought to lead first and do spreadsheets later, a retail worker helps customers first and restocks the shelves later.

Nor does it apply only to "work" in the sense of paid labor. The parent of an infant parents first, showers later. The passionate home chef cooks first, washes dishes later.

Don't procrastinate the stuff that gets at the very nature and soul of who and what you are. Prioritize that stuff. That's the stuff, after all, that matters to your heart. You'll get around to the email and the dishes later on.

"Do what makes you feel good. Give yourself authority. Realize it's a process. Breathe."

—ABENA BOAMAH-ACHEAMPONG

This right here. ***This* is how we make time our friend.** Because it's not actually time that's the enemy, it's our domination by our to-do lists.

What if, instead of fighting all the time to force ourselves to do things we don't feel like doing, we—even just once in a while—allowed excitement to dictate what we do next?

Say there are a bunch of things we need to get done. How do we decide which one to do first? Most people would say—correctly—that you do the most important thing first. That's triage, right? But how do we determine which one is the most important? Sometimes it's obvious. Some pressing matters simply must be dealt with immediately. But often, it's more open-ended.

For example, we tend to put work tasks in order by deadline—or, in the absence of deadlines, by the extent to which something is piling up and making us uncomfortable (that's one reason email tends to get so much attention and big-picture thinking so little). But you're not a task-completing robot; you're human. And that means your energy and what interests your brain vary throughout the day, from day to day.

Just finished your first cup of coffee and big thinking sounds exciting right now? Or in an afternoon slump where plowing through a pile of mindless paperwork holds a certain appeal? Both are valuable states of mind to be seized and taken advantage of while they exist.

Simply put: When we're able to give ourselves the authority to determine what's best to do next—which task our energy (or lack thereof) is drawing us toward at this moment—we do better work.

And not just better. Faster. When we're not forcing ourselves to do something we don't want to do—as if we were both reluctant schoolchild and harsh schoolmarm at the same time—we don't drag our heels so much. We zip right through whatever it is and often find we're done sooner than anticipated.

Of course, we don't always have this option. Some jobs don't afford such choices very often or at all. But *wherever* we can find room in our lives to go with the energy, we can benefit.

"I can sit down at my desk every day and do my day's work. I just do not give myself permission not to do it."

—SALMAN RUSHDIE

On the other hand, **there's a lot to be said for consistency.**

A tightly regimented schedule—where you do the same things at the same times, every time, whether you feel like it or not—can be another great tool for making time for the important stuff.

A person who swims three mornings a week whether they feel like it or not, or works on writing every Sunday afternoon whether they feel like it or not, or draws for an hour every Tuesday night whether they feel like it or not is carving out and protecting space for activities they know—in their calmest and best moments—are important to them.

Don't ask your bleary 5:30 a.m. self to make the decision about swimming, because we all know what decision that self is going to make. That self would happily pay every last dollar in your bank account for five more minutes of sleep. Instead, you're creating a structure that saves that poor self from having to make any decisions at all. The alarm goes off, sleepy-self automatically stumbles into swimsuit and sweatpants, and trundles off to the gym. Done and done.

If this seems to be directly at odds with the previous section about going where the energy is, that's because, well, basically, it is. We are smart and complicated beings and we need smart and complicated solutions to our problems. We need multiple tools in our toolboxes. Just like there's a time to cast away stones and a time to gather stones together, there's a time to follow our bliss and a time to hold ourselves to account.

Maybe a strict morning schedule where you wake up at a certain time, do certain things in a certain order, and walk out the door at a certain time on the dot is perfect for you, and maybe it's not.

Learning how and when deploying each of these differ-ent tools can help us, personally, make better friends with time—that's really the secret to the whole thing. When do you need the saw and when do you need the hammer? You will figure it out.

"Make some money and have interesting life experiences—whether that's being a teacher, or building a house, or tending a bar—keep those bills paid and write about life."

—QUIARA ALEGRIA HUDES

There's a persistent cultural message out there that if you *really* cared about your creative work, say (or about whatever it is: activism, animals, coffee, tchotchkes), you'd quit your job and go do that thing full time. We're constantly being told to take our passion and make it our livelihood.

Elizabeth Gilbert sums up the problem with this kind of thinking perfectly in her book *Big Magic:* "I've always felt like this is so cruel to your work—to demand a regular paycheck from it, as if creativity were a government job, or a trust fund . . . Financial demands can put so much pressure on the delicacies and vagaries of inspiration." Why take this precious thing you love—be it writing or art-making or baking or macramé—and insist that it now has to pay all your bills?

Once again, the culprit is our tortured perceptions of time. We fantasize that the only way to make real time, abundant time, for this thing we love is to do it all day long the way we currently do the work we get paid for.

When, in fact, if we actually made this thing our job we'd spend our days not in a blissed-out macramé haze, but rather doing quarterly taxes and email blasts and all the other things entrepreneurs must do. It would very quickly become, yep, just another day job.

Instead, how about keeping the job you have, the one that pays your rent and (we hope) provides your medical insurance, and **commit to making time for those other passions outside of working hours?**

In her piece in the *New York Times,* "Does Having a Day Job Mean Making Better Art?" Katy Waldman evokes "T. S. Eliot, conjuring 'The Waste Land' by night and overseeing foreign accounts at Lloyds Bank during the day, or Wallace Stevens, scribbling lines of poetry on his two-mile walk to work . . ."

Waldman quotes the avant-garde composer Philip Glass telling the story of a time he was recognized while doing his day job: "I suddenly heard a noise and looked up to find Robert Hughes, the art critic of *TIME* magazine, staring at me in disbelief. 'But you're Philip Glass! What are you doing here?' It was obvious that I was installing his dishwasher and I told him that I would soon be finished. 'But you are an artist,' he protested. I explained that I was an artist but that I was sometimes a plumber as well and that he should go away and let me finish."

These stories are pleasing because we recognize ourselves in them. We have bills to pay and mouths to feed, and so did all the greats of art and literature and everything else. Everyone has just 24 hours in a day to make art and make money and make anything else we want to make.

A new idiom has come into recent parlance—to "daylight in" something. Rather than "moonlighting" as a composer (with implications of scant time and secrecy), and rather than having a "day job" as a plumber (implication of onerous, meaningless labor), what if we say Philip Glass daylights in plumbing? Doesn't that sound like the sort of clear, bright, deliberate life choice a resourceful adult, with time on their side, might make?

"I capture and organize 100 percent of my 'stuff' in and with objective tools at hand, not in my mind. And that applies to *everything*— little or big, personal or professional, urgent or not. Everything."

—**DAVID ALLEN**

This is probably the single greatest insight of productivity guru Allen's popular *Getting Things Done* system (known to its adherents as GTD): the idea that **you cannot keep your tasks inside your head.** You need a system, a container to keep them in.

It doesn't really matter if that container is physical (a wire in-box or paper to-do list or bullet journal, say) or virtual (the Notes app on your phone or the Tasks function in Outlook or a dedicated program like OneNote or Evernote). What matters is that you *trust* it.

You must find the practical system that works best for you, the container you can trust, and then you must put all the things you need to do into that container. The *minute* you think of something that needs doing—pow! Into the container it goes!

This is how you stop worrying about stuff. All those things you haven't gotten around to doing yet—you don't have to keep fretting about them in your mind, reminding yourself to do them, because you trust that they are safely captured in your container.

Then, of course, you also do have to check the container periodically so you can do the things you've stored in there.

But if all the myriad stuff you need to get done is caught in one place, then that makes it super easy to grab tasks—either the most urgent ones, or the ones that fit the amount to time you happen to have at the moment—and do them. Bam!

"How we spend our days is, of course, how we spend our lives."

—ANNIE DILLARD

If we only ever put the little piddly nitpicky stuff we're in danger of forgetting onto our to-do lists—order toddler socks, pay water bill, ask Juan in Accounting about that expense report, hard-boil eggs, sign up the kids for summer camps, email the site administrator about the fundraising program, weed clothes closet, buy more paper towels, shop for anniversary gift, work on next month's client presentation, phone-bank for mayoral candidate, replace lightbulb—then those things will, quite truly and literally, take up all our available time.

Especially if we've established our trusted container— every time we have a moment to do something, we'll turn to the list in our container, grab one of these things, and do it. Which is great. Socks? Ordered! Eggs? Boiled! You are crossing things off like a to-do list champ. Go you!

Except.

Except what about the big stuff? The massive and really, really important stuff? Things like:

Get promoted. Travel to Europe. Write novel. Have baby. Get physically stronger. Change the world.

When are we going to have time for those?

This is why we have to put the big stuff—yep, even the *extremely* big stuff—on our to-do lists as well.

Sometimes this means breaking things down into just their very first step, and putting that on the list:

Book meeting to talk with boss about what it would take to get promoted.

Spend 15 minutes researching cost of plane tickets to Paris.

Schedule dinner with spouse to start talking about whether we're ready for parenthood.

But other times it means putting the whole giant goal on the list and having it recur. So every week you will work a bit on that novel, or on strength training, or on changing the world for the better.

Remember, **our to-do lists are not the boss of us.** We are the boss of them. We control what goes on them. We control how we spend our days, which means we control how we spend our lives.

And when we put the important stuff on the list, that stuff happens.

"A small daily task, if it be really daily, will beat the labors of a spasmodic Hercules."

—ANTHONY TROLLOPE

To really internalize the truth of Trollope's sentiment, to truly grasp the awesome power of small bits of time repeated frequently, all that's needed is a simple thought experiment:

To stand in for whatever the great big, daunting, seemingly impossibly large thing you personally might want to undertake is, let's use this: learning to draw.

So, say you want to learn to draw. Right now, you don't know how at all. The idea of starting, of tackling such a large project, when you are as busy as you are, seems daunting, right?

But imagine that, starting one year ago, you began setting your alarm fifteen minutes earlier on weekdays and using that time to draw. Fifteen minutes a day, five days a week, for a year. Even if we take out a couple of weeks for vacation, that's still more than sixty hours of drawing practice you'd have already had by now. You would, without question, be better at drawing at the end of the year than you were at the beginning.

People have written whole novels this way. People have started companies. People have taught themselves languages. Rekindled romances. Learned to meditate. Read the entire Harry Potter series to their children.

If we kid ourselves that big things can only be done in big chunks of time, then we sell ourselves—and our lives—impossibly short. We don't have big chunks of time, so we're basically saying big things are impossible for us. We curtail the possibility of enrichment or ambition before we've even begun.

There is a better way. Just like you can nearly always fit one more book on a crowded bookshelf, you can find or make those small pockets of time in your day. Then commit them to your big idea. And watch the magic happen.

"People set their own time. Some work 8 to 4, some work 10 to 6, some work 9 to 5."

—PATRICIA RESNICK

At the end of Patricia Resnick's film *9 to 5*, when the women take over the office, the first thing they do is institute flexible work schedules and job sharing (along with a wellness program, on-site day care, and, oh yeah, equal pay).

Forty years on, many offices are *finally* starting to get on board with the idea that **having your butt in your chair during certain specific hours on certain specific days does not necessarily map onto optimum productivity.**

There are numerous alternate schedules, but one particularly promising one is the "9/80 schedule": an employee works 80 hours in 9 days rather than 10 and then takes the tenth day off. Those every-other Fridays off then become fertile ground for personal tasks, family time, creative side-hustles, or just chilling the heck out.

"Think in the morning. Act in the noon."

—WILLIAM BLAKE

The vast majority of folks—yes, even those of us who aren't "morning people"—are **better at using our brains in the first half of the day and our bodies in the second half.** Of course, most have jobs where we must do one or the other nearly all the time. Nice as it would be to design houses in the morning, then go build them after lunch, few people get to work like that. But we can still apply this principle to good effect. For instance:

- Do all your ambitious work in the a.m., and save busywork for the p.m.

- If you have a desk job, schedule meetings for the afternoon (better yet, make them walking meetings)

- If you have a physical job (plumber, yoga teacher), reserve an hour in the morning for your planning or paperwork

- If you work on your feet (teaching, retail), don't ask yourself to do brain work (lesson planning, shift scheduling) at the day's end

"If everyone else jumped off a bridge, would you?"

—EVERYONE'S MOM, EVER

OK, so this one is controversial.

Many, many office workers—maybe even most—nowadays check work email from home at night, on the weekends, even first thing when they wake up in the morning.

That doesn't make it a good idea.

It's like your mom always said about peer pressure: Just because everyone else is doing something doesn't make that the right thing to do.

And, yes, there can be tremendous pressure to comply with these norms, especially in certain industries.

And, hey, sure, maybe you've made the conscious decision to work your butt off around the clock for a couple of years to get where you want to be. Fine.

Just don't let this be your default mode forever. Don't let it be an unexamined normal behavior.

Because, if you let it, work email can be the biggest time vacuum cleaner you ever did see. It can suck up every spare moment you might possibly be devoting to anything else that matters in your life—and even some non-"spare" moments, like ones you could be spending with your family, for instance. It will distract you, make you more anxious and less present.

If you are working, then work. If you are not working, don't work. There is no in-between land.

Of course, if you want or need to take on a second line of work—work writing that novel, work for a political candidate, work on a side-hustle for extra cash, volunteer work, house work, working out—by all means, go nuts. Evenings and weekends are the perfect chances to find those pockets of time to devote to such things.

But for the job that's paying you a paycheck? Not so much. Think about it—is that paycheck really large enough to buy *all* your time? Nope, didn't think so.

"Stop looking at the world through your cellphone screens. Have a real experience."

—ALEJANDRO GONZÁLEZ IÑÁRRITU

We all know: Mindless scrolling kills time you could spend on other, way more interesting or important things. And yet it's so alluring. **How do we fight the siren song of this little glowing rectangle that's taken over our lives? Systems!**

- A basket near the front door, alongside where you keep your keys, where everyone leaves their phones when they come home.

- A pile of phones in the middle of the table during restaurant meals with friends (they even make pouches of special shielded fabric for this—so the phones won't ring or buzz alerts).

- Phone chargers kept in the living room rather than the bedroom (plug in the phone before you retire for the night to avoid the sleep disruptions caused by looking at blue light at bedtime).

- Phone sabbath—one day a weekend when all family members agree to not use phones at all.

"Attention is the rarest and purest form of generosity."

—SIMONE WEIL

As people's lives get busier and busier, to the point where something's got to give, it can often be our friendships that take the fall. **We want to make time to see our friends, to nurture those relationships, but when everyone is busy it can be hard to make plans and even harder to keep them.** Scheduled time with pals is often the first thing to get dropped when a work or family crisis rears its head. Even though we know it's those very friends who could best bolster and support us. And we want to support them.

A regularly occurring social engagement is a great way to go. Having folks over for a monthly brunch or dinner. A recurring restaurant group or art-making club or happy-hour gang—everyone knows it's happening, no one has to waste time asking or planning. Or establish among your friends that you're always at a certain coffee shop on Saturday mornings and they should swing by and see you. Even just a regular time of day when you text your BFF might do the trick.

"We have this cultural obsession with work and productivity, as if we're better people if we don't stop and take some time for ourselves."

—ROXANE GAY

One of the great advantages of getting time on our side—of learning how to tackle our to-do lists and carve out time for the stuff that really matters—is the opportunity it affords to devote some of that newly found time to *doing nothing.*

That's right. Nothing.

As the author Roman Muradov points out in his book *On Doing Nothing,* "There is no reason to do nothing. But then, there is no reason to fall in love, or gather autumn leaves. Life reveals itself most fulsomely in gaps and intermissions."

At the end of the day, **productivity ought to gain us nonproductive time:**

Sitting at a table outside a cafe, drinking a coffee and watching the people go by.

Walking with no particular destination in mind, just looking at the world around us.

Puttering around the house, reading a book, sitting in a garden, getting an ice cream cone.

The sort of things we do when we're on vacation, instead done right in the midst of our own busy lives.

This isn't just some fantasy of sloth and idleness. Doing nothing does not mean you're lazy. On the contrary. It is both an essential refreshment for our exhausted souls and a wellspring from which comes some of the biggest, most amazing creative thinking you're ever going to do.

We don't work hard at managing our time so that we can work hard some more at managing our time some more so we can work some more so we can manage some more so we can work some more . . . No.

We work hard at managing our time so that we can rest, so we can play, so we can dream the big dreams, and love the big love, and be in the world as our own best selves.

It's a lot, this life. But, oh, it's so beautiful.

"I'm reclaiming my time."

—MAXINE WATERS

Ultimately, you decide how you spend your time. Your attention and focus and where you choose to put your energy are yours, no one else's. This is what you have.

When you "let delight pull you," like Paul Graham said way back on page 37, you're reclaiming your time.

When you stop to remember that, in the words of the artist Susan O'Malley, "you are here awake and alive," you're reclaiming your time.

When you fight for what is right in the spirit of congresswoman and badass Maxine Waters, you're reclaiming your time.

This is how we make time meaningful and not just something to be slogged through. Love. Joy. Mindfulness. Justice.

Take a minute. Find your time. Reclaim it.

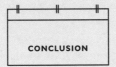

CONCLUSION

Time is not the enemy. The writer Tara Rodden Robinson once said, "I came to realize that the entire field of personal productivity is rooted in this lie of scarcity . . . But the truth is: Time is an infinitely renewable and inexhaustibly abundant resource."

When you first read Robinson's words, you will probably want to punch someone in the face. Even after all we've talked about in this book, it would be pretty amazing if you didn't.

"Time isn't abundant and infinite," you want to shout. "Time is finite! That's just the nature of time!"

Maybe not on a cosmic scale, but on the scale of a human lifetime, yes, you're right. We all only get so many hours, so many days and months and years. Then we die. The fact that we all, without exception, are going to drop dead someday is a big part of what drives us to race around in circles trying to do everything all at once all the time.

But it's also a big part of what makes our lives, and the years and the months and the weeks and the days and the hours and the teeny-tiny fulsome minutes in them, so deeply, achingly, heartbreakingly precious and beautiful.

If we weren't ever going to croak, could we ever know how good we have it? How miraculous existence is compared to nonexistence?

And this is where we start, slowly at first and then with increasing speed and momentum, to grasp Robinson's point. Because we have so so *so* much. Maybe sometimes too much. We have abundance in all directions. And when did a scarcity mind-set ever get anyone anywhere except straight to miserable?

Thinking of time as the enemy—as a scarce, slippery, mean, and meager little thing dribbling away through our fingers—is a recipe for unhappiness.

Trusting that time can be our friend—**that we have the tools and the resources and the smarts and the bigness of heart to *choose* to view time as abundant**—well, that's a recipe for plenty.

Making friends with time is *not* mind over matter, which is nonsense. It's not effort over circumstances, which is privileged nonsense. It's a commitment. It's faith in our own capabilities. And, in a way, it's faith in the Earth's transit around the sun.

Days will pass. There's nothing we can do about that. Indeed—given the alternative—there's no way we'd want to do anything about that.

Stuff will need to get done. And, again—given the alternative—we don't want to change that either.

How we choose to spend our days, how we choose to spend our spare quarter hours, what we decide to prioritize, *who* we decide to prioritize, how we view this maelstrom of a world and our place in it . . .

That's up to us.

ACKNOWLEDGMENTS

Thank you to my delightful editor, pal, and work-wife, Christina Amini, for bringing to fruition my long-held dream of writing "the time book." Thank you to the very fine people of Chronicle Books, including—but not limited to—Dena Rayess, Michele Posner, Rachel Harrell, Janine Sato, Sarah Lin Go, and Diane Levinson. Vast and eternal gratitude to all the folks who shared their stories with me for All the Stuff We Need to Do: Tiffanie, Erin, Shweta, Kate, Lisa C., Bryant, Kristen W. E., Christina, Ana, Bruno, Joel, Jen, Benjamin, Matthew, Deanne, Andrea, Allison, Wynn, Lisa A., Jenn, Mirabelle, Alan, Bill, Tiffany, Vanessa, Rachael, Brian, Rae, Katharine, Rebecca, Kathy, Lisa S., Tess, Sheila, Kristen H., Maurice, Maggi, Casey, Kelly, Ginee, Kim, and Stephen— this book would be radically diminished without your openness. Thank you to my parents for their perpetual love and support in all things I do. And huge thanks to Bill and Mabel for being the very best thing I get to make time for.

Allen, David. *Getting Things Done: The Art of Stress-Free Productivity.* New York: Penguin, 2001.

Barker, Eric. "This Is How to Be Productive: 5 New Secrets Proven by Research." Barking Up the Wrong Tree (blog). http://www.bakadesuyo.com/2016/07/how-to-be-productive/.

Blake, William. *The Marriage of Heaven and Hell.* Mineola, NY: Dover, 1994.

Boamah-Acheampong, Abena. "On Anxiety." Talk for Creative Mornings (speaker series). http://www.creativemornings.com/talks/abena-boamah-acheampong/1.

Brontë, Charlotte. *Villette.* Oxford: Oxford University Press, 1990.

Coates, Ta-Nehisi. "Ask Ta-Nehisi Anything." TheAtlantic.com. http://www.theatlantic.com/notes/2017/01/on-trump-and-the-election/513017/.

Coates, Ta-Nehisi. "The Case for Reparations." In *We Were Eight Years in Power: An American Tragedy.* New York: One World, 2017.

Comedy Central and J. Rentilly. "The Secret to Foreplay, According to Tracy Morgan." MensHealth.com. http://www.menshealth.com/trending-news/a19533811/tracy-morgan.

Davis, Lydia. "What You Learn about the Baby." In *The Collected Stories of Lydia Davis*. New York: Picador, 2009.

Dillard, Annie. *The Writing Life*. New York: Harper Perennial, 2013.

Fragoso, Sam. "Janelle Monáe: NASA's Black Women in *Hidden Figures* 'Made America Great Again.'" The Complex. http://www.complex.com/pop-culture/2016/12/janelle-monae-hidden-figures-moonlight-interview.

Galchen, Rivka. *Little Labors*. New York: New Directions, 2016.

Gay, Roxane, and Abigail Bereola. "The Rumpus Interview with Roxane Gay." The Rumpus. http://www.therumpus.net/2017/01/the-rumpus-interview-with-roxane-gay/.

Gilbert, Elizabeth. *Big Magic: Creative Living Beyond Fear*. New York: Riverhead, 2015.

Glei, Jocelyn K. *Hurry Slowly* (podcast). Episode 15, "Oliver Burkeman—Against Time Management." January 30, 2018. http://www.hurryslowly.co/015-oliver-burkeman/.

Glei, Jocelyn K. *Unsubscribe: How to Kill Email Anxiety, Avoid Distractions, and Get Real Work Done*. New York: Public Affairs, 2016.

Graham, Paul. "Good and Bad Procrastination" (blog). http://www.paulgraham.com/procrastination.html.

Han, Tiffany. "A Year of Truth Talks 72/365" (Instagram series). http://www.instagram.com/p/BgSRnjAnL9X/.

Harris, Kamala, and Dayo Olopade. "Kamala Harris, the 'Female Obama,' Wins Primary for California Attorney General." The Daily Beast. http://www.thedailybeast.

com/kamala-harris-the-female-obama-wins-primary-
for-california-attorney-general.

Hudes, Quiara Alegria, and Beth Stevens. "Quiara Alegria
Hudes on Why She Wrote Daphne's Dive and How
Lin-Manuel Miranda Is Like Seinfeld's Kramer." Broadway.
com. http://www.broadway.com/buzz/184898/
quiara-alegria-hudes-on-why-she-wrote-daphnes-
dive-how-lin-manuel-miranda-is-like-seinfelds-kramer/.

Iñárritu, Alejandro González, Armando Bo, Alexander
Dinelaris, and Nicolás Giacobone. *Birdman* (film). Los
Angeles: Fox Searchlight, 2014.

McGuinness, Mark. "Getting Unstuck." In *Manage Your
Day-to-Day: Build Your Routine, Find Your Focus, and
Sharpen Your Creative Mind* by 99U, edited by Jocelyn K.
Glei. Las Vegas: Amazon Publishing, 2013.

Messinger, Ruth. "Justice as a Spiritual Practice: 2009 Stanford
Baccalaureate Remarks." https://news.stanford.edu/
news/2009/june17/messinger_text-061709.html.

Miranda, Lin-Manuel. *Hamilton: The Revolution*. New York:
Grand Central, 2016.

Morrison, Toni. *Jazz*. New York: Alfred A. Knopf, 1992.

Muradov, Roman. *On Doing Nothing: Finding Inspiration in
Idleness*. San Francisco: Chronicle Books, 2018.

Obama, Barack. "Barack Obama's Feb. 5 Speech."
NYTimes.com. http://www.nytimes.com/2008/02/05/us/
politics/05text-obama.html.

O'Connor, Anahad. "How to Start Working Out." NYTimes. com. http://www.nytimes.com/guides/smarterliving/ how-to-start-exercising.

Oliver, Mary. *Upstream: Selected Essays*. New York: Penguin, 2016.

O'Malley, Susan. *A Healing Walk* (art installation). Saratoga, CA: Montalvo Arts Center. http://www.susanomalley.org/a-healing-walk/.

Penny, Louise. *The Long Way Home*. New York: Minotaur Books, 2014.

Pitney, Nico. "The Awkward Black Girl Who Is Going to Change Television." Huffington Post. http://www. huffingtonpost.com/2015/04/15/awkward-black-girl_n_7035808.html.

Rao, Srinivas. "Why Having a System is Essential to Increasing Your Creative Output." The Mission (blog). http://www.medium.com/the-mission/why-having-a-system-is-essential-to-increasing-your-creative-output-12feae92de66.

Resnick, Patricia, and Colin Higgins. *9 to 5* (film). Los Angeles: Twentieth Century Fox, 1980.

Rhimes, Shonda. *Year of Yes: How to Dance It Out, Stand in the Sun, and Be Your Own Person*. New York: Simon and Schuster, 2016.

Robinson, Tara Rodden, and Lisa Congdon. "Tara Rodden Robinson on Productivity." Today Is Going to Be Awesome (blog). http://www.lisacongdon.com/blog/2016/04/tara-rodden-robinson/.

Ruhl, Sarah. *100 Essays I Don't Have Time to Write*. New York: Farrar, Straus, and Giroux, 2014.

Rushdie, Salman, and Alison Beard. "Salman Rushdie on Creativity and Criticism." *Harvard Business Review* (online). http://www.hbr.org/ideacast/2015/08/salman-rushdie-on-creativity-and-criticism.html.

Sbarra, David. "I Trained Myself to Be Less Busy—And It Dramatically Improved My Life." Vox.com. http://www.vox.com/first-person/2017/1/25/14362156/busy-overwhelmed-values.

Scarry, Richard. *What Do People Do All Day?* New York: Random House, 1968.

Schulte, Brigid. *Overwhelmed: Work, Love, and Play When No One Has the Time*. New York: Picador, 2014.

Shapiro, Rami. *Wisdom of the Jewish Sages: A Modern Reading of the Pirke Avot*. New York: Harmony / Bell Tower, 1995.

Trollope, Anthony. *An Autobiography*. Oxford: Oxford University Press, 2009.

Waldman, Katy. "Does Having a Day Job Mean Making Better Art?" *New York Times*, March 22, 2018. http://www.nytimes.com/2018/03/22/t-magazine/art/artist-day-job.html.

Walker, Alice, and Pratibha Parmar. *Alice Walker: Truth in Beauty* (film). Berkeley, CA: Kali Films, 2013.

Waters, Maxine. Comments made during the House Financial Services Committee hearing with treasury secretary Steve Mnuchin, July 27, 2017.

(continued)

http://www.c-span.org/video/?431675-1/treasury
-secretary-testifies-state-international-finance-system.

Webb, Eileen. "Productivity in Terrible Times." The Human
in the Machine (blog). http://www.superyesmore.com/
productivity-in-terrible-times-709d4b3127
845e2d090bf94f0b93263.

Weil, Simone. *First and Last Notebooks.* Translated by
R. Rees. Oxford: Oxford University Press, 1970.

White, E. B. *Here Is New York.* New York: The Little Book
Room, 1999.

Whyte, David. *The Three Marriages: Reimagining Work, Self,
and Relationships.* New York: Riverhead, 2010.

Williams, Venus. "Interview with Venus Williams."
CNN.com. http://www.cnn.com/2008/WORLD/
asiapcf/01/23/talkasia.venus/index.html.

Winfrey, Oprah, and J.J. McCorvey. "The Key to Oprah
Winfrey's Success: Radical Focus." *Fast
Company.* https://www.fastcompany.com/3051589/
the-key-to-oprah-winfreys-success-radical-focus.

Wolf, Michelle. *Nice Lady* (television special). New York:
HBO, 2017.